WITHDRAWN

COOPERATIVE LIBRARY SERVICES

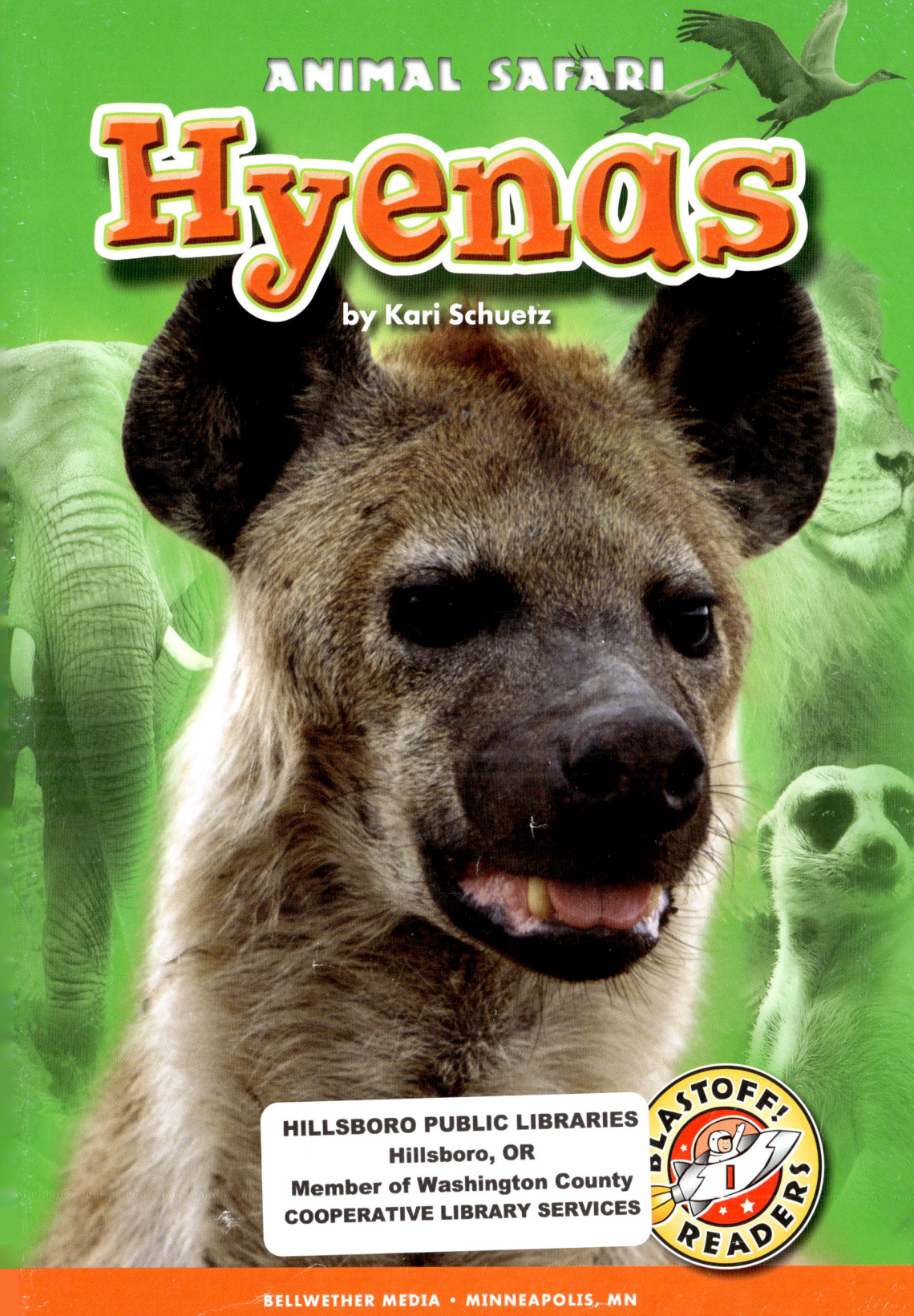

Animal Safari
Hyenas

by Kari Schuetz

BELLWETHER MEDIA • MINNEAPOLIS, MN

Note to Librarians, Teachers, and Parents:

Blastoff! Readers are carefully developed by literacy experts and combine standards-based content with developmentally appropriate text.

Level 1 provides the most support through repetition of high-frequency words, light text, predictable sentence patterns, and strong visual support.

Level 2 offers early readers a bit more challenge through varied simple sentences, increased text load, and less repetition of high-frequency words.

Level 3 advances early-fluent readers toward fluency through increased text and concept load, less reliance on visuals, longer sentences, and more literary language.

Level 4 builds reading stamina by providing more text per page, increased use of punctuation, greater variation in sentence patterns, and increasingly challenging vocabulary.

Level 5 encourages children to move from "learning to read" to "reading to learn" by providing even more text, varied writing styles, and less familiar topics.

Whichever book is right for your reader, Blastoff! Readers are the perfect books to build confidence and encourage a love of reading that will last a lifetime!

This edition first published in 2012 by Bellwether Media, Inc.

No part of this publication may be reproduced in whole or in part without written permission of the publisher. For information regarding permission, write to Bellwether Media, Inc., Attention: Permissions Department, 5357 Penn Avenue South, Minneapolis, MN 55419.

Library of Congress Cataloging-in-Publication Data

Schuetz, Kari.
 Hyenas / by Kari Schuetz.
     p. cm. – (Blastoff! readers. Animal safari)
 Includes bibliographical references and index.
 Summary: "Developed by literacy experts for students in kindergarten through grade three, this book introduces hyenas to young readers through leveled text and related photos"–Provided by publisher.
 ISBN 978-1-60014-717-3 (hardcover : alk. paper)
 1. Hyenas–Juvenile literature. I. Title.
QL737.C24S38 2012
599.74'3–dc23
                                    2011031238

Text copyright © 2012 by Bellwether Media, Inc. BLASTOFF! READERS and associated logos are trademarks and/or registered trademarks of Bellwether Media, Inc. SCHOLASTIC, CHILDREN'S PRESS, and associated logos are trademarks and/or registered trademarks of Scholastic Inc.

Printed in the United States of America, North Mankato, MN.
010112   1207

Contents

What Are Hyenas?	4
Clans	8
Scavenging	14
Hunting	16
Glossary	22
To Learn More	23
Index	24

What Are Hyenas?

Hyenas are **mammals** with hunched backs. Their front legs are longer than their back legs.

Hyenas have powerful **jaws**. Their strong teeth can crush bones.

Clans

Hyenas roam **savannahs** in groups called **clans**. One clan can have up to 80 hyenas.

A female hyena is the leader of a clan. She is called the **alpha female**.

The alpha female leads group hunts. She also gives birth to most of the clan's **cubs**.

Scavenging

Hyenas **scavenge** for food. They eat the meat, skin, and bones of dead animals.

Hunting

Many hyenas also hunt for food. They chase zebras, antelopes, and other animals.

These hyenas laugh when they catch their **prey**. This calls other hyenas to come eat.

The noise also attracts other **predators**. Lions often try to steal a hyena's kill. Food fight!

Glossary

alpha female—the female hyena that leads a clan

clans—groups of hyenas that live together

cubs—young hyenas

jaws—the bones that form the mouths of some animals

mammals—warm-blooded animals that have backbones and feed their young milk

predators—animals that hunt other animals for food

prey—animals that are hunted by other animals for food

savannahs—grasslands with few trees

scavenge—to find and eat dead animals

To Learn More

AT THE LIBRARY

Grucella, Ethan. *Hyenas*. New York, N.Y.: Gareth Stevens Pub., 2011.

Hadithi, Mwenye. *Hungry Hyena*. London, U.K.: Hodder and Stoughton, 1994.

Sierra, Judy. *The Mean Hyena: A Folktale from Malawi*. New York, N.Y.: Lodestar Books, 1997.

ON THE WEB

Learning more about hyenas is as easy as 1, 2, 3.

1. Go to www.factsurfer.com.

2. Enter "hyenas" into the search box.

3. Click the "Surf" button and you will see a list of related Web sites.

With factsurfer.com, finding more information is just a click away.

Index

alpha female, 10, 12
antelopes, 16
birth, 12
bones, 6, 14
calls, 18
chase, 16
clans, 8, 10, 12
crush, 6
cubs, 12
hunched backs, 4
hunts, 12, 16
jaws, 6
kill, 20
laugh, 18
legs, 4
lions, 20
mammals, 4
meat, 14
predators, 20
prey, 18
roam, 8
savannahs, 8
scavenge, 14
skin, 14
teeth, 6
zebras, 16

The images in this book are reproduced through the courtesy of: Werner Bollmann / Age Fotostock, front cover; Henry Wilson, pp. 5, 17 (right); Ann and Steve Toon / Alamy, pp. 7, 19; Michel Bureau / Photolibrary, p. 9; Gerard Soury / Photolibrary, p. 11; Mike Wilkes / npl / Minden Pictures p. 13; Jeremy Woodhouse / Masterfile, p. 15; Juniors Bildarchiv / Alamy, p. 17 (top); Mogens Trolle, p. 17 (left); Michel & Christine Denis-Huot / Biosphoto, p. 21.